The Revenge of the Flower Arrangers

Also by Dave Walker and available from Canterbury Press

The Dave Walker Colouring Book

Heroes of the Coffee Rota

Peculiar Goings On

The Exciting World of Church Going

The Dave Walker Guide to the Church

My Pew: Things I Have Seen from It

How to Avoid the Peace

www.canterburypress.co.uk

The Revenge of the Flower Arrangers

Dave Walker

CANTERBURY
PRESS
Norwich

© Dave Walker 2019

First published in 2019 by the Canterbury Press Norwich
Editorial office
3rd Floor, Invicta House
108–114 Golden Lane
London EC1Y 0TG, UK
www.canterburypress.co.uk

Canterbury Press is an imprint of Hymns Ancient & Modern Ltd (a registered charity)

Hymns Ancient & Modern® is a registered trademark of Hymns Ancient & Modern Ltd
13A Hellesdon Park Road, Norwich,
Norfolk NR6 5DR, UK

British Library Cataloguing in Publication data

A catalogue record for this book is available
from the British Library

978 1-78622-231 2

Printed and bound in Great Britain by
CPI Group (UK) Ltd

GOING TO A NEW CHURCH

SOME QUESTIONS

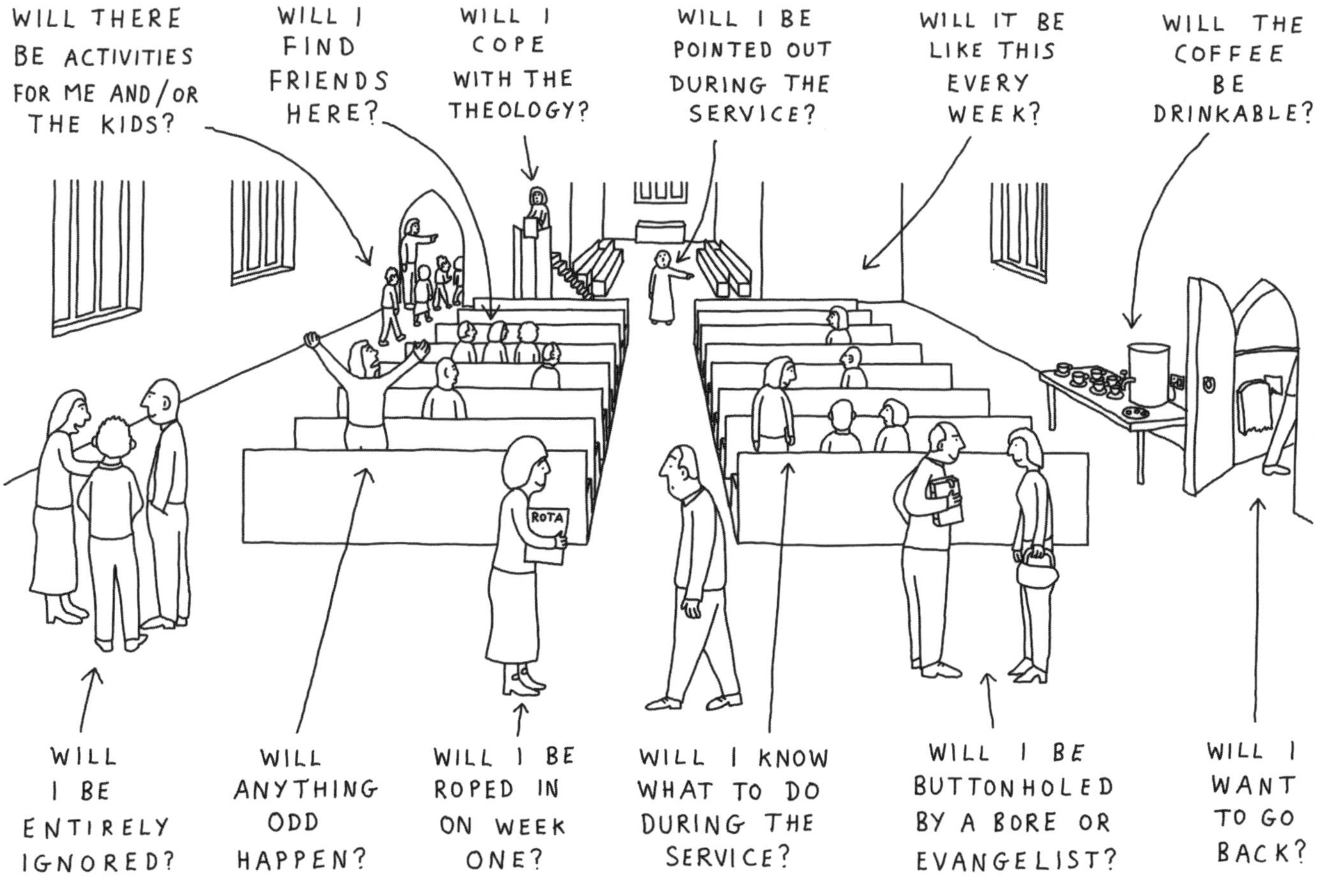
WILL THERE BE ACTIVITIES FOR ME AND/OR THE KIDS?
WILL I FIND FRIENDS HERE?
WILL I COPE WITH THE THEOLOGY?
WILL I BE POINTED OUT DURING THE SERVICE?
WILL IT BE LIKE THIS EVERY WEEK?
WILL THE COFFEE BE DRINKABLE?
ROTA
WILL I BE ENTIRELY IGNORED?
WILL ANYTHING ODD HAPPEN?
WILL I BE ROPED IN ON WEEK ONE?
WILL I KNOW WHAT TO DO DURING THE SERVICE?
WILL I BE BUTTONHOLED BY A BORE OR EVANGELIST?
WILL I WANT TO GO BACK?

THE GUIDES

WILL SHOW YOU AROUND

THE TOWER

THE PAINTINGS

THE WINDOWS

THE MONUMENTAL BRASSES

THE CRYPT

THE EXHAUSTED CLERGY

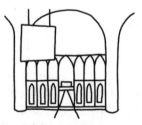

THE SCREEN

THE DONATION BOX

SHEETS OF PAPER

PLEASE MAKE SURE YOU HAVE THE CORRECT ONE TO HAND

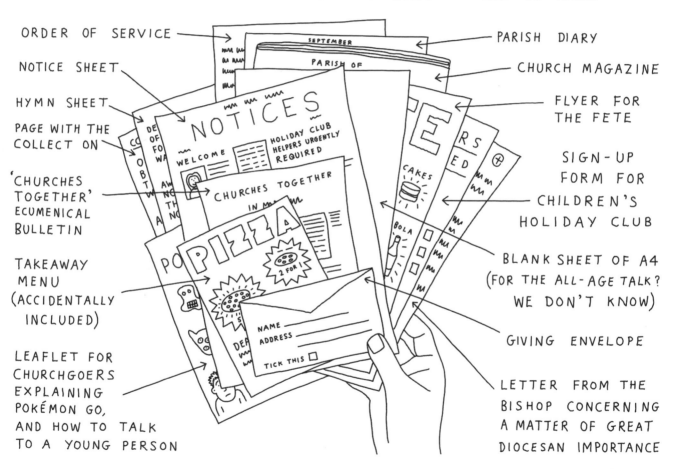

ORDER OF SERVICE

NOTICE SHEET

HYMN SHEET

PAGE WITH THE COLLECT ON

'CHURCHES TOGETHER' ECUMENICAL BULLETIN

TAKEAWAY MENU (ACCIDENTALLY INCLUDED)

LEAFLET FOR CHURCHGOERS EXPLAINING POKÉMON GO, AND HOW TO TALK TO A YOUNG PERSON

PARISH DIARY

CHURCH MAGAZINE

FLYER FOR THE FETE

SIGN-UP FORM FOR CHILDREN'S HOLIDAY CLUB

BLANK SHEET OF A4 (FOR THE ALL-AGE TALK? WE DON'T KNOW)

GIVING ENVELOPE

LETTER FROM THE BISHOP CONCERNING A MATTER OF GREAT DIOCESAN IMPORTANCE

HAND SIGNALS

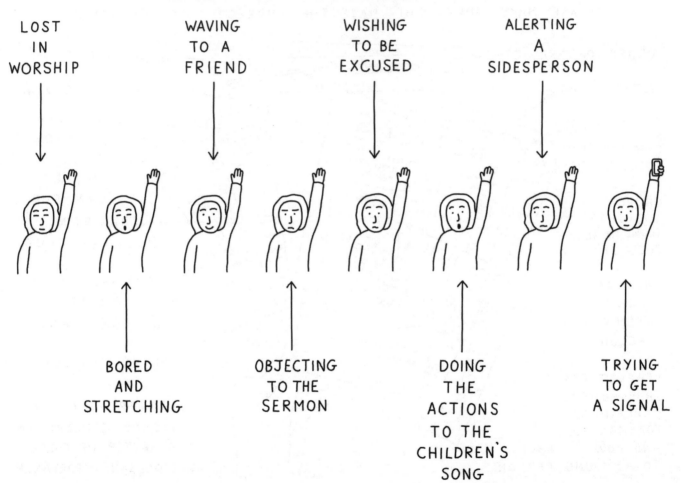

LOST
IN
WORSHIP

WAVING
TO A
FRIEND

WISHING
TO BE
EXCUSED

ALERTING
A
SIDESPERSON

BORED
AND
STRETCHING

OBJECTING
TO THE
SERMON

DOING
THE
ACTIONS
TO THE
CHILDREN'S
SONG

TRYING
TO GET
A SIGNAL

A TIME OF SILENCE

PLEASE IGNORE ALL DISTRACTIONS

COUGHING

SNEEZING

SNIFFING

YAWNING

WHISPERING

RUSTLING

RUMMAGING

LAWNMOWERS

THE MICROPHONE (FEEDBACK)

THE SUNDAY SCHOOL (MISC. NOISES)

THE URN (BOILING)

THE TRAFFIC

THE PERSON AT THE FRONT DESCRIBING, AT SOME LENGTH, THE BENEFITS OF A TIME OF SILENCE, BEFORE EXPLAINING VARIOUS PRACTICALITIES

SIDESPERSONS WHO THINK THEY CAN'T BE HEARD

MINOR INCIDENTS INVOLVING HYMN BOOKS

THE ALL-AGE TALK

HOW TO GET THE CROWD ON YOUR SIDE

DANGER

CHOCOLATE

PROPS

PYROTECHNICS

AN ELEMENT OF COMPETITION

AN ANIMAL

AWKWARD SILENCE

A JOKE

TECHNICIANS TRYING TO MAKE IT WORK

A VIDEO

QUEUE TO BUY DOWNLOAD OF TALK

BEING INCREDIBLY INTERESTING

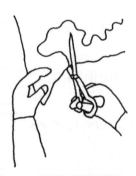

ASKING PEOPLE TO DO SOME CUTTING OUT

SERMONS

POPULAR COMPLAINTS

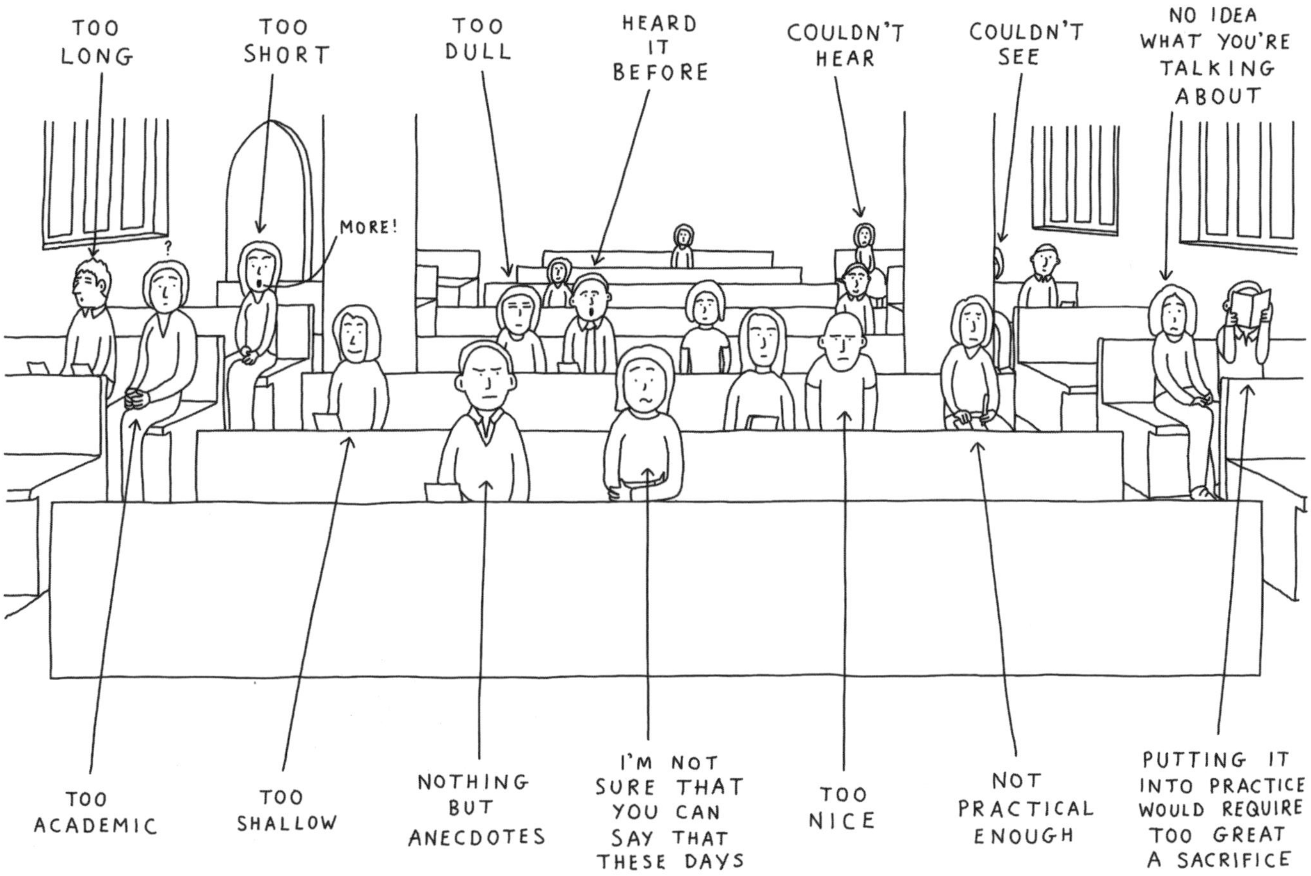

TOO LONG
TOO SHORT
MORE!
TOO DULL
HEARD IT BEFORE
COULDN'T HEAR
COULDN'T SEE
NO IDEA WHAT YOU'RE TALKING ABOUT
TOO ACADEMIC
TOO SHALLOW
NOTHING BUT ANECDOTES
I'M NOT SURE THAT YOU CAN SAY THAT THESE DAYS
TOO NICE
NOT PRACTICAL ENOUGH
PUTTING IT INTO PRACTICE WOULD REQUIRE TOO GREAT A SACRIFICE

PREACHING A SERMON

COMBINE ANY OF THE FOLLOWING

FASCINATING ANECDOTES

A HILARIOUS JOKE

WHAT THE GREEK SAYS

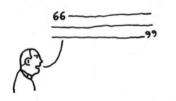

INSPIRATIONAL QUOTES

**REFERENCES TO
TOPICAL GOINGS-ON**

**WHAT THE BIBLE
PASSAGE REALLY MEANS**

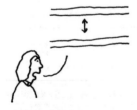

FILLER

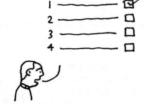

PRACTICAL APPLICATION

**INCREDIBLY VAGUE CONCLUSION
THAT WON'T UPSET ANYONE**

SHARING THE PEACE

HANDSHAKE

HUG

BADGE
SHOWING
WHERE
CONTACTLESS
IS
ACCEPTED

PEW ETIQUETTE

WHEN GOING UP FOR COMMUNION

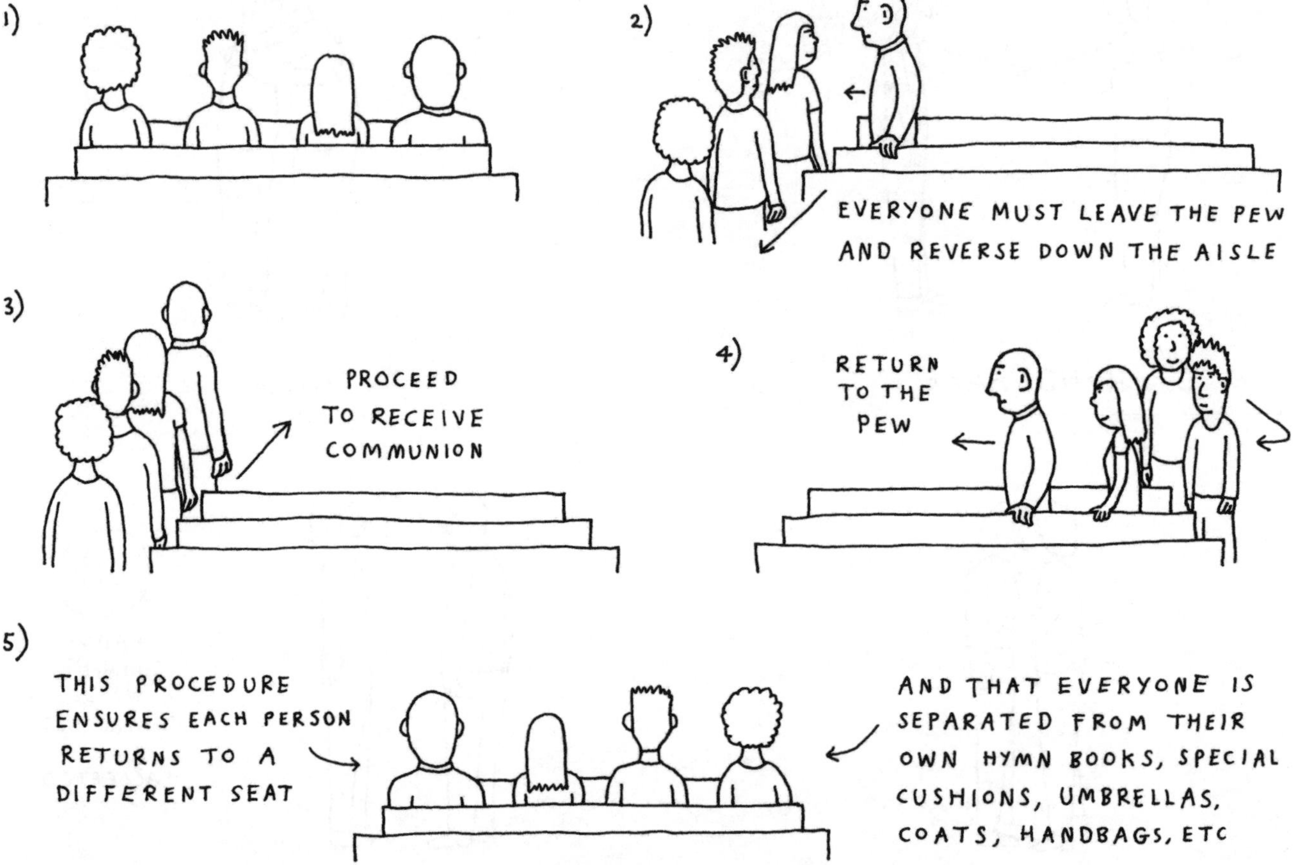
1)
2)
EVERYONE MUST LEAVE THE PEW AND REVERSE DOWN THE AISLE
3)
PROCEED TO RECEIVE COMMUNION
4)
RETURN TO THE PEW
5)
THIS PROCEDURE ENSURES EACH PERSON RETURNS TO A DIFFERENT SEAT
AND THAT EVERYONE IS SEPARATED FROM THEIR OWN HYMN BOOKS, SPECIAL CUSHIONS, UMBRELLAS, COATS, HANDBAGS, ETC

NEIGHBOURS

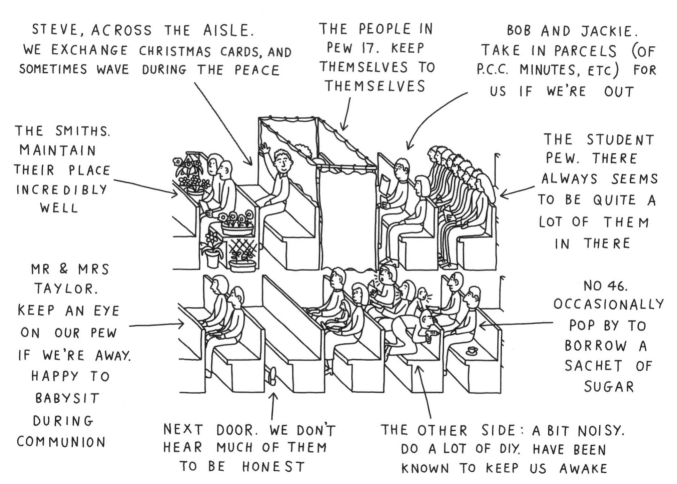

STEVE, ACROSS THE AISLE. WE EXCHANGE CHRISTMAS CARDS, AND SOMETIMES WAVE DURING THE PEACE

THE PEOPLE IN PEW 17. KEEP THEMSELVES TO THEMSELVES

BOB AND JACKIE. TAKE IN PARCELS (OF P.C.C. MINUTES, ETC) FOR US IF WE'RE OUT

THE SMITHS. MAINTAIN THEIR PLACE INCREDIBLY WELL

THE STUDENT PEW. THERE ALWAYS SEEMS TO BE QUITE A LOT OF THEM IN THERE

MR & MRS TAYLOR. KEEP AN EYE ON OUR PEW IF WE'RE AWAY. HAPPY TO BABYSIT DURING COMMUNION

NO 46. OCCASIONALLY POP BY TO BORROW A SACHET OF SUGAR

NEXT DOOR. WE DON'T HEAR MUCH OF THEM TO BE HONEST

THE OTHER SIDE: A BIT NOISY. DO A LOT OF DIY. HAVE BEEN KNOWN TO KEEP US AWAKE

INITIATION

PARTICIPATE IN A
CATECHUMENAL COURSE

[WORD FOUND
ON THE INTERNET]

LEARN AND
RECITE THE
HEALTH AND
SAFETY POLICY

WADE BLINDFOLDED THROUGH THE
OBSTACLE-STREWN FLOODED CRYPT

THE SASH
OF
BELONGING

THE SWORD
OF
WELCOME

THE CUP
OF
TEA

ATTEND A
SPECIAL CEREMONY
(DETAILS VARY
BY DENOMINATION)

MAY WE PASS YOUR
DETAILS ON TO OTHER
CAREFULLY-SELECTED
DENOMINATIONS? ☑

SIGN:

SIGN THE PAPERWORK

FLOWERS   COFFEE   STANDING
AROUND
HELPLESSLY
AT THE
YOUTH CLUB,
TRYING
DESPERATELY
TO MAINTAIN
SOME
SEMBLANCE
OF ORDER

CLEAN   MOVING
CHAIRS
AROUND

JOIN SOME ROTAS

A CHAT WITH THE VICAR

HOW TO AVOID VOLUNTEERING FOR ANYTHING

EXPLAIN ABOUT MANY AND VARIED FAMILY RESPONSIBILITIES

OUTLINE SHEER INCOMPETENCE WHEN IT COMES TO LEADING THINGS

SHOW HOW FULL YOUR DIARY IS

EXTOL THE VIRTUES OF OTHERS

DEMONSTRATE INABILITY TO MAKE TEA

FEIGN AN INJURY

SAY NO

OUTREACH

OUR MISSION ACTION PLAN

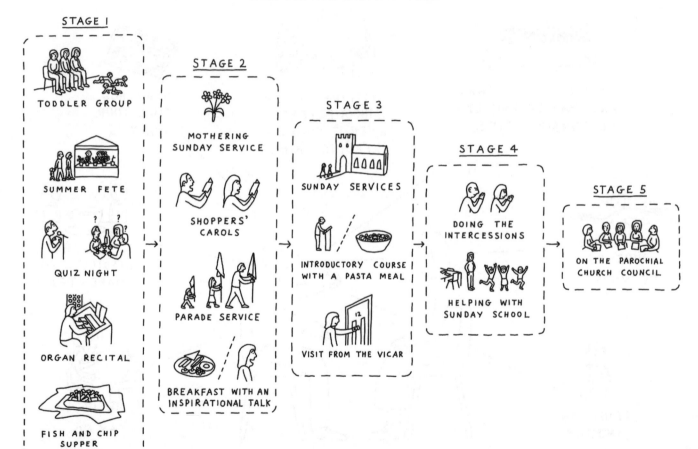

STAGE 1
- TODDLER GROUP
- SUMMER FETE
- QUIZ NIGHT
- ORGAN RECITAL
- FISH AND CHIP SUPPER

STAGE 2
- MOTHERING SUNDAY SERVICE
- SHOPPERS' CAROLS
- PARADE SERVICE
- BREAKFAST WITH AN INSPIRATIONAL TALK

STAGE 3
- SUNDAY SERVICES
- INTRODUCTORY COURSE WITH A PASTA MEAL
- VISIT FROM THE VICAR

STAGE 4
- DOING THE INTERCESSIONS
- HELPING WITH SUNDAY SCHOOL

STAGE 5
- ON THE PAROCHIAL CHURCH COUNCIL

CUPS AND SAUCERS

WHEN THEY ARE RETURNED TO THE KITCHEN

NEW PERSON WHO NO ONE SPOKE TO

THE MAJORITY OF THE CONGREGATION

RECIPIENTS OF THE DISAPPOINTING EARLY BATCH OF LUKEWARM COFFEE

CUP AND SAUCER MYSTERIOUSLY ABANDONED ON A DISTANT PEW

FLOWER ARRANGER MAKING POST-SERVICE REVISIONS

THE VICAR, DEALING WITH A PASTORAL EMERGENCY

NUMBER OF CUPS AND SAUCERS

0   5   10   15   20   25   30   35   40   45   50   55   1 HOUR

TIME AFTER END OF SERVICE

SKILLS

GAINED OVER A LIFETIME OF CHURCHGOING

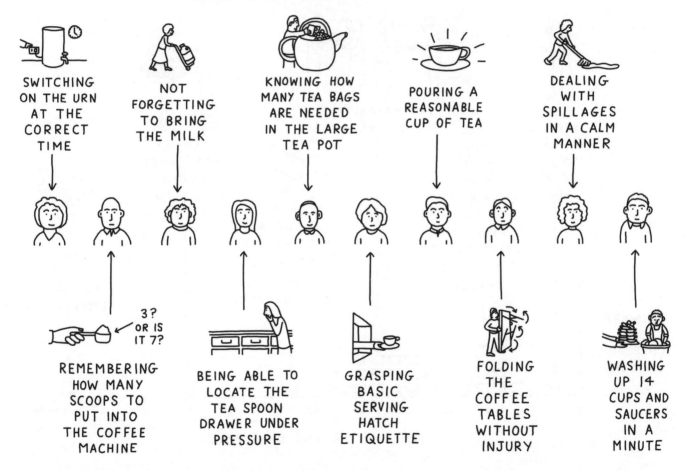

SWITCHING ON THE URN AT THE CORRECT TIME

NOT FORGETTING TO BRING THE MILK

KNOWING HOW MANY TEA BAGS ARE NEEDED IN THE LARGE TEA POT

POURING A REASONABLE CUP OF TEA

DEALING WITH SPILLAGES IN A CALM MANNER

3? OR IS IT 7?

REMEMBERING HOW MANY SCOOPS TO PUT INTO THE COFFEE MACHINE

BEING ABLE TO LOCATE THE TEA SPOON DRAWER UNDER PRESSURE

GRASPING BASIC SERVING HATCH ETIQUETTE

FOLDING THE COFFEE TABLES WITHOUT INJURY

WASHING UP 14 CUPS AND SAUCERS IN A MINUTE

AUTOMATION

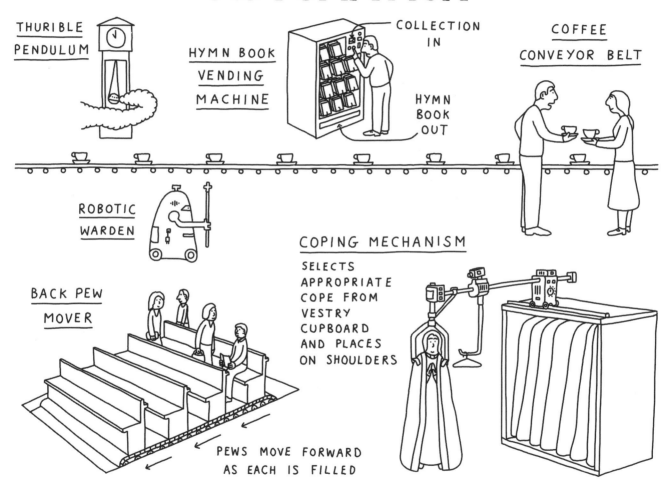

THURIBLE PENDULUM

HYMN BOOK VENDING MACHINE

COLLECTION IN

HYMN BOOK OUT

COFFEE CONVEYOR BELT

ROBOTIC WARDEN

COPING MECHANISM

SELECTS APPROPRIATE COPE FROM VESTRY CUPBOARD AND PLACES ON SHOULDERS

BACK PEW MOVER

PEWS MOVE FORWARD AS EACH IS FILLED

PEWS
ALTERNATIVE USES

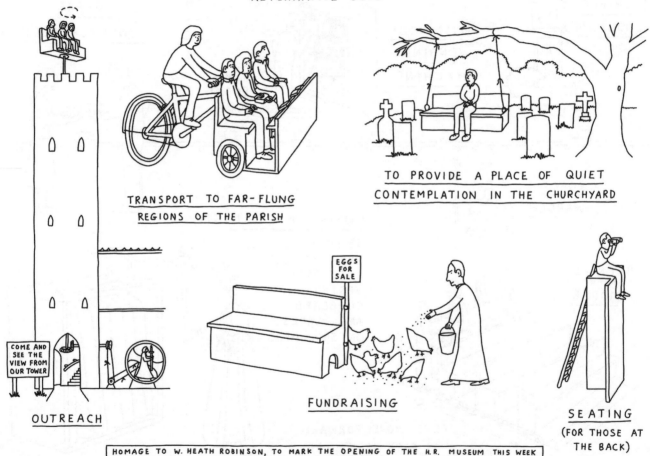

TRANSPORT TO FAR-FLUNG
REGIONS OF THE PARISH

TO PROVIDE A PLACE OF QUIET
CONTEMPLATION IN THE CHURCHYARD

COME AND
SEE THE
VIEW FROM
OUR TOWER

EGGS
FOR
SALE

OUTREACH

FUNDRAISING

SEATING
(FOR THOSE AT
THE BACK)

HOMAGE TO W. HEATH ROBINSON, TO MARK THE OPENING OF THE H.R. MUSEUM THIS WEEK

CHURCH SEATING

DEVELOPMENT OVER TIME

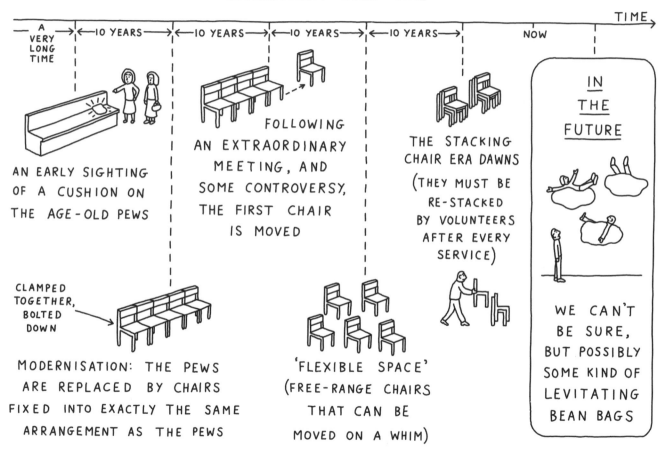

TIME

A VERY LONG TIME | 10 YEARS | 10 YEARS | 10 YEARS | 10 YEARS | NOW

AN EARLY SIGHTING OF A CUSHION ON THE AGE-OLD PEWS

FOLLOWING AN EXTRAORDINARY MEETING, AND SOME CONTROVERSY, THE FIRST CHAIR IS MOVED

THE STACKING CHAIR ERA DAWNS (THEY MUST BE RE-STACKED BY VOLUNTEERS AFTER EVERY SERVICE)

IN THE FUTURE

CLAMPED TOGETHER, BOLTED DOWN

MODERNISATION: THE PEWS ARE REPLACED BY CHAIRS FIXED INTO EXACTLY THE SAME ARRANGEMENT AS THE PEWS

'FLEXIBLE SPACE' (FREE-RANGE CHAIRS THAT CAN BE MOVED ON A WHIM)

WE CAN'T BE SURE, BUT POSSIBLY SOME KIND OF LEVITATING BEAN BAGS

VESTMENTS

CLERGY ADJUST TO THE FACT THAT ROBES ARE NOW OPTIONAL

FRESH EXPRESSIONS OF
MINISTERIAL STYLE EMERGE

RESISTANCE FROM THOSE WHO
SEE VESTMENTS AS MISSIONAL

CLERGY OUTFITTERS CONTINUE
TO TOUR THEOLOGICAL COLLEGES

THE DIOCESE RUNS
A COURSE

COPES

AND THE HOME FURNISHINGS THAT INSPIRED THEM

CINCTURES

THEIR USES

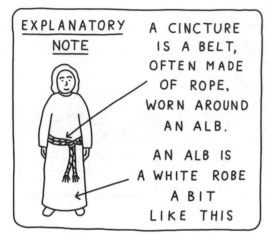

EXPLANATORY NOTE

A CINCTURE IS A BELT, OFTEN MADE OF ROPE, WORN AROUND AN ALB.

AN ALB IS A WHITE ROBE A BIT LIKE THIS

EMERGENCY DOG LEAD

BELL ROPE

TO SUSPEND A THURIBLE

CROWD-CONTROL BARRIER

TO RESCUE THOSE IN PERIL IN THE FONT

DRONES
ECCLESIASTICAL USES

TAKING UP THE
COLLECTION

SURVEYING THE
CHURCH ROOF

DELIVERING NEWSLETTERS
AROUND THE PARISH

CHECKING UP ON
THE NEIGHBOURS

PUTTING THE STAR ON THE
CHURCH CHRISTMAS TREE

SEARCH AND
RESCUE

THE CHURCH WEBSITE

WHY CAN'T WE HAVE THE PROPER TUNE?

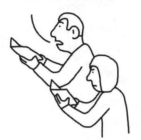

COME ON - THE QUICKER WE MOVE THESE CHAIRS THE QUICKER WE CAN ALL GO HOME

REBRANDING THE CHURCH

HOW TO DESIGN A NEW LOGO

HOLD A
MEETING

SEE WHETHER ANYONE HAS
A NIECE OR NEPHEW WHO KNOWS
ABOUT THIS KIND OF THING

LET THE
SUNDAY SCHOOL
HAVE A GO

LOOK IN A
BOOK OF FONTS

APPOINT A COMMITTEE TO
THRASH OUT THE DETAIL

UNVEIL THE FINAL DESIGN
AT THE 10AM SERVICE

THE CHURCH WORK PARTY

THEIR TASKS

MOW THE CHURCHYARD

THAT WAS THE AREA WE WERE REWILDING!

TRIM SOME BRANCHES

THAT WAS GOING TO BE NEXT YEAR'S CHRISTMAS TREE!

PULL DOWN THE DILAPIDATED SHED NEXT TO THE CHURCH

THAT WAS THE CHURCH HALL!

GO INSIDE FOR A COFFEE

THAT WAS THE BIT I'VE JUST DONE!

FUNDRAISING

EVENT IDEA GENERATOR

THE VICAR / YOUTH GROUP / CONGREGATION / CHOIR / FLOWER ARRANGERS

IS/ARE RUNNING / ABSEILING / LIVING IN A TENT / SELLING CAKES / CRAWLING

FOR 100 MILES / 24 HOURS / A MONTH / AS LONG AS IT TAKES / EVER

WHILST WEARING FANCY DRESS / SINGING ALL OF THE HYMNS / TELLING JOKES / JUGGLING / RATTLING A TIN

PLEASE DONATE / SPONSOR / PURCHASE A RAFFLE TICKET / BUY TEA AND A CAKE / STAY AWAY

OUTREACH

MORE BRILLIANT IDEAS

ADD LOTS OF GLASS SO THAT ONLOOKERS
WILL BE DESPERATE TO COME IN

BE ACTIVE ON SOCIAL MEDIA

INFILTRATE THE PILATES GROUP
THAT HIRES THE CHURCH HALL

GO OUT INTO THE COMMUNITY

THE NEIGHBOURS

1. COMPLAIN ABOUT THE BELLS
2. COMPLAIN ABOUT THE UNSIGHTLY BINS
3. COMPLAIN ABOUT PARKING
4. COMPLAIN ABOUT KIDS MAKING A NOISE
5. COMPLAIN ABOUT LOUD SINGING

NEIGHBOURS WHO HAVE BEEN THERE LONGER THAN THE CHURCH, OR WHO WERE UNAWARE OF IT WHEN THEY MOVED IN:

NO RESULTS FOUND

THE CRYPT
POSSIBLE USES

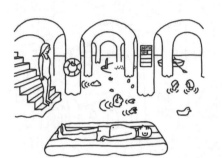

SWIMMING POOL

VICAR'S WINE CELLAR

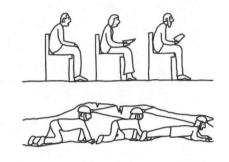

POTHOLING CENTRE

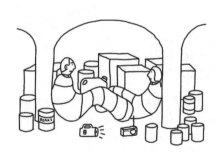

NUCLEAR BUNKER

MUSEUM OF CHURCH HEATING

DUNGEON

THE GRAVEYARD

REASONS TO SUBMIT A COMPLAINT TO THE VICAR

THE GRASS HASN'T BEEN CUT

THERE ARE OBJECTS ON THE GRAVES

THE GRASS HAS BEEN CUT

THE OBJECTS HAVE BEEN REMOVED

SMALL CONGREGATIONS
VARIOUS STRATEGIES

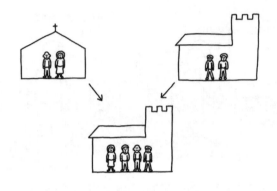

AMALGAMATION

PARISH OF WWWWW
SUNDAY SERVICE 10AM
CHILDCARE
WIFI FOR HOMEWORKERS
POST OFFICE
LAWNMOWERS SERVICED WHILE YOU WAIT

DIVERSIFICATION

CONVINCING THE CHURCH AUTHORITIES
THAT EVERYTHING IS ABSOLUTELY FINE

CARRYING ON AS NORMAL

THE NEW EXTENSION

IT WILL MAKE
THE BUILDING
FAR MORE FRIENDLY
AND WELCOMING

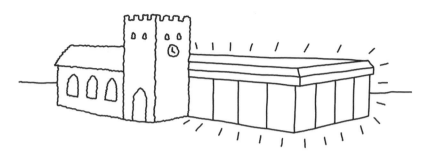

RULES

NO
BISCUITS
IN
THE
COFFEE
LOUNGE

NO
OUTSIDE
SHOES
INSIDE

THIS WAY
BISHOP

WASH
HANDS
AT
ALL
TIMES

DON'T USE
HANDS
TO OPEN
GLASS
DOORS

STICKY
FINGER-
PRINTS

CHAIRS ONLY TO
BE STACKED BY
THOSE WHO HAVE
COMPLETED THE
TRAINING COURSE

NO
CRAFT
ACTIVITIES
WITHOUT
A PERMIT

GLITTER

THE BALLOON
WAYS TO RETRIEVE IT FROM THE RAFTERS

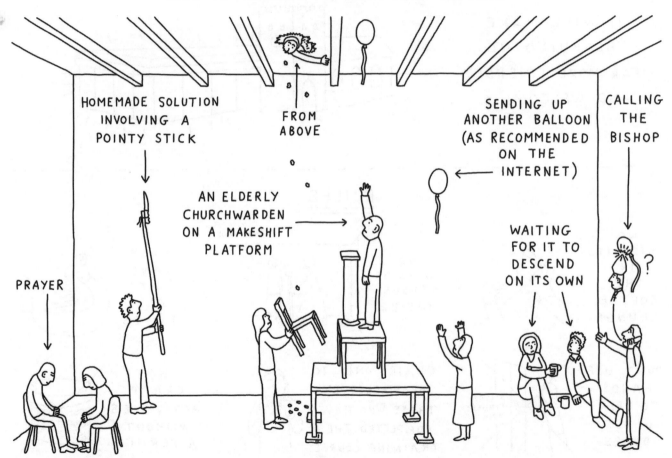

HOMEMADE SOLUTION INVOLVING A POINTY STICK

FROM ABOVE

SENDING UP ANOTHER BALLOON (AS RECOMMENDED ON THE INTERNET)

CALLING THE BISHOP

AN ELDERLY CHURCHWARDEN ON A MAKESHIFT PLATFORM

PRAYER

WAITING FOR IT TO DESCEND ON ITS OWN

THE FLOWER ARRANGERS

WHAT THEY DO DURING LENT

RELAX

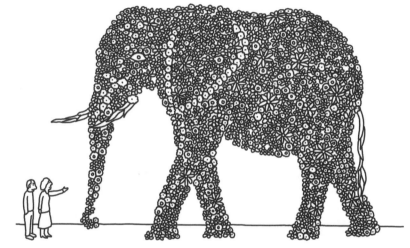

UNDERTAKE PRIVATE COMMISSIONS

MAKE PLANS
FOR CHRISTMAS

JET BACK FOR
MOTHERING SUNDAY

PARTY

LENT BOOKS

SEVEN DEADLY SINS

SLOTH

GREED

PRIDE

GLUTTONY

ENVY

LUST

WRATH

THE ANNUAL MEETING

INTERESTING REPORTS ABOUT KEY
AREAS OF OUR WORK

THE VICAR'S SPEECH ABOUT
THIS YEAR'S ACHIEVEMENTS

THE ELECTION OF A NEW
PAROCHIAL CHURCH COUNCIL

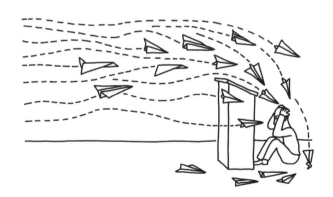

SOME QUESTIONS FROM
CONGREGATION MEMBERS

EASTER

WHAT'S ON OFFER?

A WIDE VARIETY
OF CARDS, ALL
OF WHICH ARE A
SHADE OF
PALE YELLOW

2 FOR 1
ON
ALL
CHOCOLATE
EGGS

EXTRA 20%
OFF EVERYTHING
DISPLAYING
THE BUNNY
SYMBOL

POETRY,
MUSIC,
SALVATION,
COFFEE

THE EASTER EGG HUNT

PARENTS WHO WERE, IN HINDSIGHT, TOO EAGER TO GIVE THEIR CHILD A COMPETITIVE ADVANTAGE

THE SUNDAY CLUB LEADER, WHOSE JOB IT IS TO MAKE A PROFOUND SPIRITUAL POINT

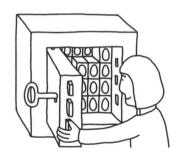

HIDDEN VESTRY EGG STASH, TO SUSTAIN THE CLERGY THROUGH THE LONG MONTHS OF ORDINARY TIME

ECCLESIASTICAL AUTHORITIES, MAKING SURE THAT THE EVENT IS CORRECTLY NAMED

EASTER
THINGS WE CAN NOW DO

GO ON HOLIDAY (CLERGY)

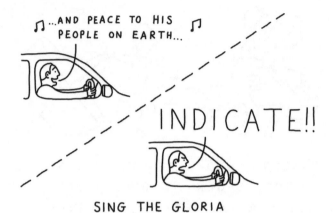

SING THE GLORIA

DISPLAY FLOWERS

EAT AND DRINK FORBIDDEN TREATS

THE CHURCH WEEKEND AWAY

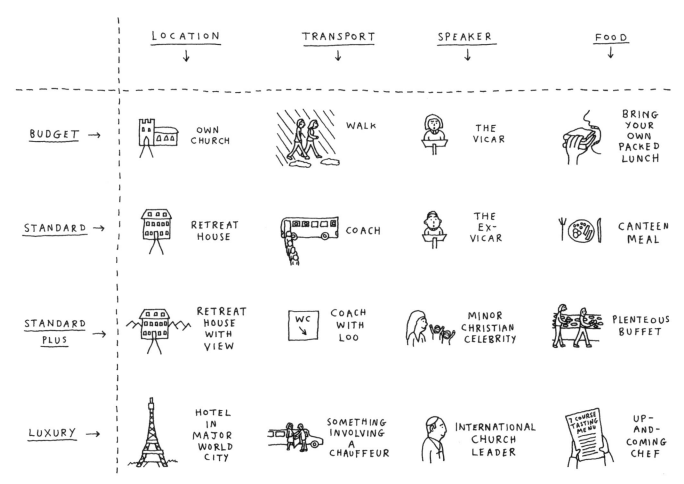

	LOCATION ↓	TRANSPORT ↓	SPEAKER ↓	FOOD ↓
BUDGET →	OWN CHURCH	WALK	THE VICAR	BRING YOUR OWN PACKED LUNCH
STANDARD →	RETREAT HOUSE	COACH	THE EX-VICAR	CANTEEN MEAL
STANDARD PLUS →	RETREAT HOUSE WITH VIEW	COACH WITH LOO	MINOR CHRISTIAN CELEBRITY	PLENTEOUS BUFFET
LUXURY →	HOTEL IN MAJOR WORLD CITY	SOMETHING INVOLVING A CHAUFFEUR	INTERNATIONAL CHURCH LEADER	UP-AND-COMING CHEF

THE CAKE STALL

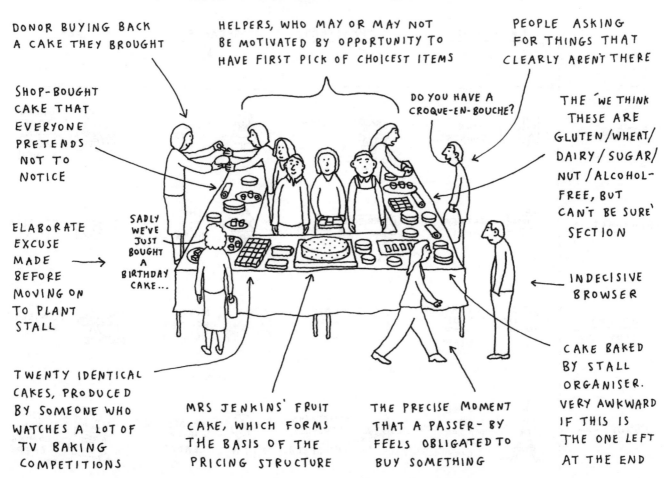

DONOR BUYING BACK A CAKE THEY BROUGHT

HELPERS, WHO MAY OR MAY NOT BE MOTIVATED BY OPPORTUNITY TO HAVE FIRST PICK OF CHOICEST ITEMS

PEOPLE ASKING FOR THINGS THAT CLEARLY AREN'T THERE

SHOP-BOUGHT CAKE THAT EVERYONE PRETENDS NOT TO NOTICE

DO YOU HAVE A CROQUE-EN-BOUCHE?

THE 'WE THINK THESE ARE GLUTEN/WHEAT/DAIRY/SUGAR/NUT/ALCOHOL-FREE, BUT CAN'T BE SURE' SECTION

ELABORATE EXCUSE MADE BEFORE MOVING ON TO PLANT STALL

SADLY WE'VE JUST BOUGHT A BIRTHDAY CAKE...

INDECISIVE BROWSER

TWENTY IDENTICAL CAKES, PRODUCED BY SOMEONE WHO WATCHES A LOT OF TV BAKING COMPETITIONS

MRS JENKINS' FRUIT CAKE, WHICH FORMS THE BASIS OF THE PRICING STRUCTURE

THE PRECISE MOMENT THAT A PASSER-BY FEELS OBLIGATED TO BUY SOMETHING

CAKE BAKED BY STALL ORGANISER. VERY AWKWARD IF THIS IS THE ONE LEFT AT THE END

THE HOLIDAYS

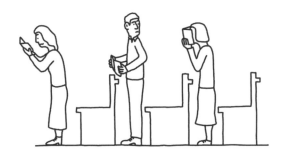

THE RELIEF ORGANIST PLAYS
TUNES WE DON'T REALLY KNOW

BUT MY PEW
IS OVER THERE

THE COVER CHURCHWARDEN DIRECTS
PEOPLE TO UNEXPECTED SEATS

THE TEMPORARY FLOWER ARRANGER
CREATES CHALLENGING DISPLAYS

THE VISITING SIDESPERSON TOOK
THE COLLECTION, AND WAS
NEVER SEEN AGAIN

43

RITUALS

FOR HOT WEATHER

THE BRINGING FORTH
OF THE FANS

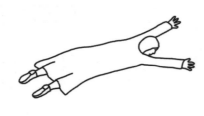

PROSTRATION ON A
COLD MARBLE FLOOR

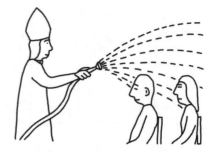

HOSEPIPE SPRINKLING

INSPECTION OF THE
COLD WATER TANK
BY FULL IMMERSION

MEDITATION IN
THE CRYPT

THE GIVING OF
AN ICED LOLLY

AUGUST

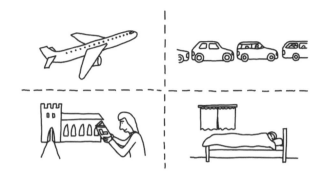

THE MINISTRY TEAM HAVE
GONE ON HOLIDAY

THE 10 A.M. SERVICE HAS BEEN LEFT
IN A BOX FOR THE CONGREGATION

HYMNS   PRAYERS   ALL-AGE TALK   SERMON   AFTER-SERVICE COFFEE   PASTORAL CARE   SENSE OF MYSTERY

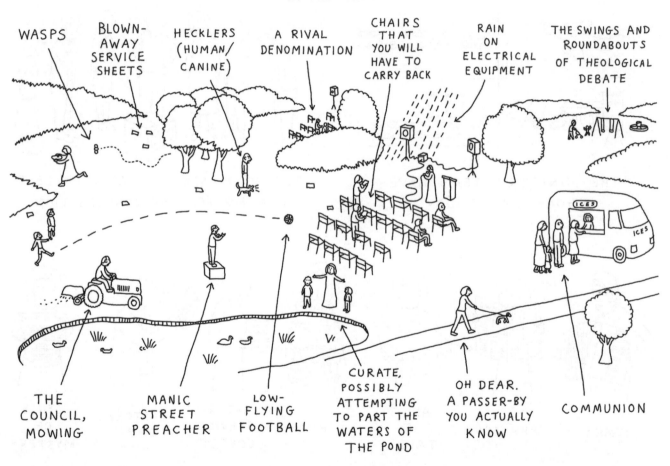

THE SUMMER SERVICE

IN THE PARK

WASPS

BLOWN-AWAY SERVICE SHEETS

HECKLERS (HUMAN/CANINE)

A RIVAL DENOMINATION

CHAIRS THAT YOU WILL HAVE TO CARRY BACK

RAIN ON ELECTRICAL EQUIPMENT

THE SWINGS AND ROUNDABOUTS OF THEOLOGICAL DEBATE

THE COUNCIL, MOWING

MANIC STREET PREACHER

LOW-FLYING FOOTBALL

CURATE, POSSIBLY ATTEMPTING TO PART THE WATERS OF THE POND

OH DEAR. A PASSER-BY YOU ACTUALLY KNOW

COMMUNION

ICES

CHILDREN

WAYS TO KEEP THEM AMUSED DURING THE SUMMER MONTHS

THEME PARKS

ART

THE COUNTRYSIDE

TRAVEL

ICE CREAM

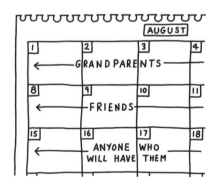

LENDING THEM OUT

THE SUMMER FESTIVAL

SHOULD WE GO, OR STAY AT HOME?

<u>GO</u>

<u>STAY</u>

BRILLIANT ENTERTAINMENT

SEEING FRIENDS

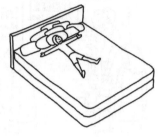

TOILETS AND SHOWERS

AN ACTUAL BED

A CHANCE TO WEAR FESTIVAL CLOTHES

IT MIGHT NOT RAIN TOO MUCH

HOME COOKING

THERE MIGHT BE SOMETHING ON TV

48

ADVENT

CONTROVERSIES

WHO WILL LIGHT THE CANDLES
ON THE ADVENT WREATH?

SHOULD THE WREATH HAVE
ONE PINK CANDLE?

WHETHER TO PREACH ON
CHALLENGING ADVENT THEMES

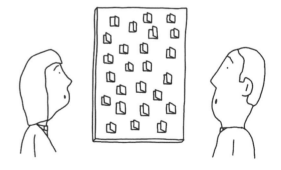

WHO COULD HAVE EATEN THE
VESTRY ADVENT CALENDAR CHOCOLATES?

THE CLERGY DIARY

DECEMBER (APPROXIMATE)

1 CHRISTMAS TREE MANOEUVRES

2  UNEARTHING CRIB SCENE FROM DEPTHS OF STORAGE

3 CHILDPROOFING CHURCH BEFORE SCHOOL VISITS

4 BLESSING THE TREE IN THE HIGH STREET

5 SETTING THE HEATING FOR EVERY SINGLE EVENT

6 WRITING INSPIRATIONAL REFLECTIONS FOR NUMEROUS CAROL SERVICES

7 ORGANISING MULTIPLE READERS FOR NUMEROUS CAROL SERVICES

8 NUMEROUS CAROL SERVICES

9  RISK-ASSESSING DONKEY IN NATIVITY PLAY

10   RATHER MORE FUNERALS THAN USUAL

11 DRESSING UP AS AN ANGEL

12 SOURCING 500 ORANGES

13 VISITING THOSE FOR WHOM CHRISTMAS IS A DIFFICULT TIME

14 FITTING IN A HAIR CUT

15 HOSTING P.C.C. DRINKS

16  REMOVING GLITTER FROM BLACK TROUSERS

17 REMOVING WAX FROM JUST ABOUT EVERYTHING

18 BUYING MINCE PIES, BECAUSE THE VOLUNTEERS FORGOT TO

19 REMEMBERING TO BUY PRESENTS FOR FAMILY MEMBERS

20 GARGLING WHISKY TO KEEP VOICE

21 MAKING NOTE TO BE MORE ORGANISED NEXT YEAR

22 CALLING OUT A PHOTOCOPIER MECHANIC

23 CHECKING THAT THE BABY JESUS HASN'T BEEN REPLACED BY A TEDDY BEAR

24 LIGHTING HUNDREDS OF TEA LIGHTS

25 DASHING SOMEWHERE FOR LUNCH AFTER CHRISTMAS MORNING SERVICES

26 COLLAPSING IN A HEAP

27 PLANNING EASTER SERVICES

28,29,30,31 HIBERNATING

THE CHRISTMAS MARKET

KNITTED MISCELLANY STALL

LEGENDARY MARMALADE STALL

INAPPROPRIATE PAPERBACK STALL

WREATHS THAT MAY OR MAY NOT MAKE IT THROUGH ADVENT

PARTNER BEING ENCOURAGED TO BUY GIFT

MULLED LIQUID, INGREDIENTS UNKNOWN

PAYING TO GET IN

DONATED ITEMS THAT WON'T SELL (UNDER TABLE)

TOMBOLA MADE UP OF LAST YEAR'S UNWANTED PRESENTS

GIFTS BEING SOLD FOR SLIGHTLY LESS THAN THEY COST TO MAKE

ELDERLY MEN WITH BAD BACKS FROM CARRYING TABLES

PAYING TO GET OUT

THE SCHOOL CAROL SERVICE

YEAR 8 VISIT THE PARISH CHURCH

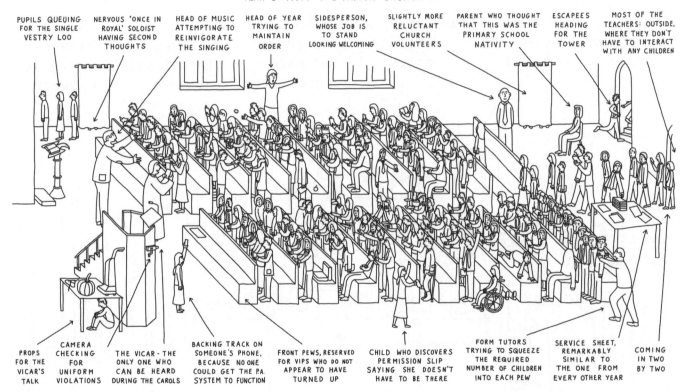

PUPILS QUEUING FOR THE SINGLE VESTRY LOO

NERVOUS 'ONCE IN ROYAL' SOLOIST HAVING SECOND THOUGHTS

HEAD OF MUSIC ATTEMPTING TO REINVIGORATE THE SINGING

HEAD OF YEAR TRYING TO MAINTAIN ORDER

SIDESPERSON, WHOSE JOB IS TO STAND LOOKING WELCOMING

SLIGHTLY MORE RELUCTANT CHURCH VOLUNTEERS

PARENT WHO THOUGHT THAT THIS WAS THE PRIMARY SCHOOL NATIVITY

ESCAPEES HEADING FOR THE TOWER

MOST OF THE TEACHERS: OUTSIDE, WHERE THEY DON'T HAVE TO INTERACT WITH ANY CHILDREN

PROPS FOR THE VICAR'S TALK

CAMERA CHECKING FOR UNIFORM VIOLATIONS

THE VICAR - THE ONLY ONE WHO CAN BE HEARD DURING THE CAROLS

BACKING TRACK ON SOMEONE'S PHONE, BECAUSE NO ONE COULD GET THE P.A. SYSTEM TO FUNCTION

FRONT PEWS, RESERVED FOR VIPS WHO DO NOT APPEAR TO HAVE TURNED UP

CHILD WHO DISCOVERS PERMISSION SLIP SAYING SHE DOESN'T HAVE TO BE THERE

FORM TUTORS TRYING TO SQUEEZE THE REQUIRED NUMBER OF CHILDREN INTO EACH PEW

SERVICE SHEET, REMARKABLY SIMILAR TO THE ONE FROM EVERY OTHER YEAR

COMING IN TWO BY TWO

THE CHURCH CHRISTMAS TREE

PITFALLS TO AVOID

TOO BIG

TOO SMALL

DECORATING ISSUES

NEEDLES DROPPING

INCORRECT PLACEMENT

RESISTANCE FROM
THE CONGREGATION

UNWANTED CHRISTMAS PRESENTS

DONATE THEM TO YOUR LOCAL CHURCH

JUMPERS

FOOD

TOILETRIES

HUMOUR BOOKS

SCARVES

SCENTED CANDLES

THE WINTER GAMES

AT YOUR LOCAL CHURCH

SNOWBOARDING

SKI JUMPING

TRAY FROM THE CHURCH KITCHEN

THE CURATE IS VOLUNTEERED TO HAVE FIRST GO

SKELETON

CHURCH CAR PARK (UNTREATED)

SPEED SKATING

SHINY CHURCH HALL FLOOR

KNEELER

THE PARISH VACUUM CLEANER

CURLING

SLALOM

THE CHURCH HEATING SYSTEM

THE ECCLESIASTICAL DETECTIVE

THE DETECTIVE

THE VICAR

THE SIDEKICK

THE PARISH ADMINISTRATOR

THE NEMESIS

THE ORGANIST

THIS WEEK'S CRIME SCENE

THE CHURCH HALL: SOMEONE HAS BEEN LARKING AROUND WITH THE TODDLER-GROUP TOYS

SUSPECTS

THE YOUNG PEOPLE

THE FLOWER ARRANGERS

THE KEEP FIT GROUP

THE CHURCH CAT

CLUES

A CONSTANT DRIPPING FROM THE GUTTERING

A MUSTY HYMN BOOK AROMA

THE AGENDA FROM A RECENT P.C.C. MEETING

THE LID REMOVED FROM THE PARISH BISCUIT TIN

CHURCHWARDENS' WANDS

THEY HAVE SEVERAL FUNCTIONS

CEREMONIAL

PRACTICAL

MUSICAL

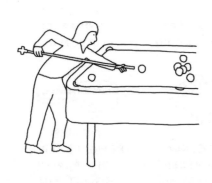

SOCIAL

ANTISOCIAL

MAGICAL

TRAINING

FOR CARRYING A GREAT BIG LONG STICK IN CHURCH

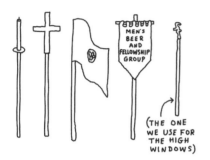

ANYONE CARRYING ONE OF THESE ITEMS MUST ENROL ON AN IN-DEPTH TRAINING COURSE

THIS INCLUDES MANY HOURS ON A HAZARD SIMULATOR

A LECTURE SERIES BY LEARNED EXPERTS

THERE IS AN EXAM

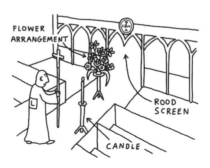

AND FINALLY A PRACTICAL TEST

SUCCESSFUL STUDENTS ARE COMMISSIONED BY THE BISHOP AT A SPECIAL CATHEDRAL SERVICE

THE P.C.C.

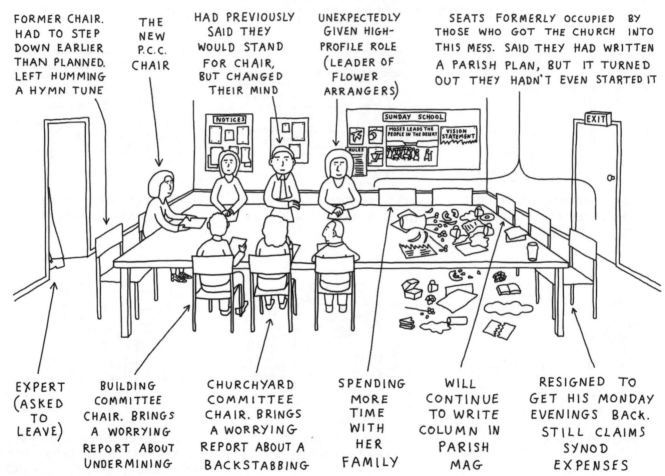

FORMER CHAIR. HAD TO STEP DOWN EARLIER THAN PLANNED. LEFT HUMMING A HYMN TUNE

THE NEW P.C.C. CHAIR

HAD PREVIOUSLY SAID THEY WOULD STAND FOR CHAIR, BUT CHANGED THEIR MIND

UNEXPECTEDLY GIVEN HIGH-PROFILE ROLE (LEADER OF FLOWER ARRANGERS)

SEATS FORMERLY OCCUPIED BY THOSE WHO GOT THE CHURCH INTO THIS MESS. SAID THEY HAD WRITTEN A PARISH PLAN, BUT IT TURNED OUT THEY HADN'T EVEN STARTED IT

NOTICES

SUNDAY SCHOOL

MOSES LEADS THE PEOPLE IN THE DESERT

VISION STATEMENT

RULES

EXIT

EXPERT (ASKED TO LEAVE)

BUILDING COMMITTEE CHAIR. BRINGS A WORRYING REPORT ABOUT UNDERMINING

CHURCHYARD COMMITTEE CHAIR. BRINGS A WORRYING REPORT ABOUT A BACKSTABBING

SPENDING MORE TIME WITH HER FAMILY

WILL CONTINUE TO WRITE COLUMN IN PARISH MAG

RESIGNED TO GET HIS MONDAY EVENINGS BACK. STILL CLAIMS SYNOD EXPENSES

THE CHURCH ADMINISTRATOR

THEIR DUTIES

STAFF THE CONTROL
ROOM IN THE TOWER

PUT THE RESERVATION
TICKETS ON THE PEWS

KNOW WHERE THE CLERGY
ARE AT ALL TIMES

MAKE SURE THE SERVICE
SHEETS ARE DISTRIBUTED

ARRANGE FOR BROKEN
THINGS TO BE FIXED

STAND IN FOR LAST-
MINUTE ROTA ABSENTEES

THE STATIONERY CUPBOARD

IN THE CHURCH OFFICE

SOMEWHERE INSIDE, YOU MAY BE ABLE TO FIND:

PASTEL PAPER FOR THE PARISH MAGAZINE COVER

MANY DIFFERENT BRANDS OF PAPER, BOUGHT IN THE HOPE OF FINDING JUST ONE THAT DOESN'T JAM THE COPIER

GLOSSY LEAFLETS, PRINTED DURING THE TIMES OF PLENTY

TEMPLATE FOR VICAR'S LETTERS TO ECCLESIASTICAL NEWSPAPER

INSPIRATIONAL NOTICE-BOARD POSTERS, BOUGHT, BUT LATER REGRETTED

COPIES OF SOME OF THE VERY IMPORTANT FORMS

HEADED NOTEPAPER WITH THE OLD E-MAIL ADDRESS

'SORRY I MISSED YOU' CARDS

'SECRETLY QUITE GLAD I MISSED YOU' CARDS

PLANNED GIVING ENVELOPES

UNPLANNED GIVING ENVELOPES

READY-MADE SIGNS PROHIBITING ILLEGAL PARKING/ PEW OCCUPATION

CONFIDENTIALITY

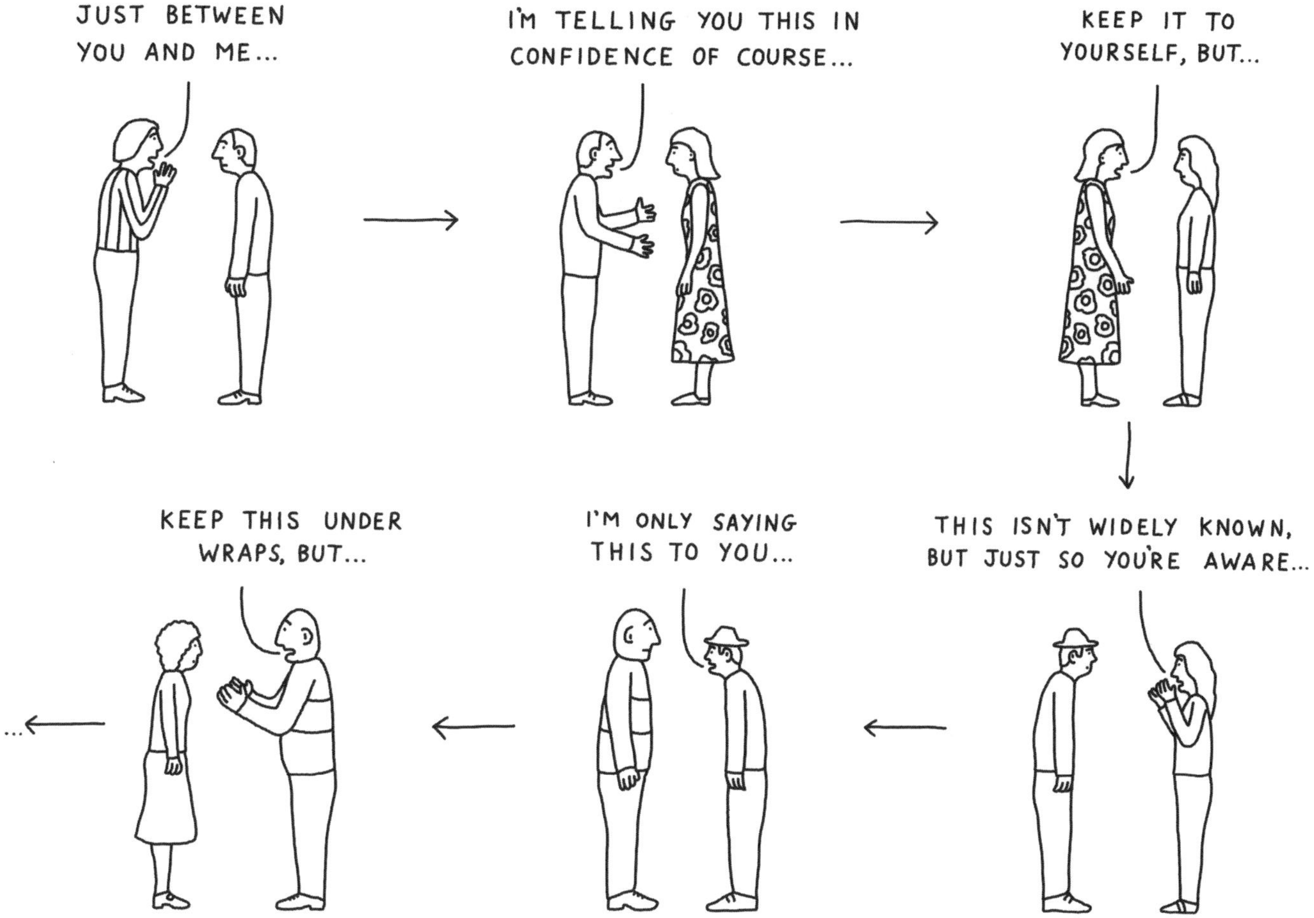
JUST BETWEEN YOU AND ME...
I'M TELLING YOU THIS IN CONFIDENCE OF COURSE...
KEEP IT TO YOURSELF, BUT...
THIS ISN'T WIDELY KNOWN, BUT JUST SO YOU'RE AWARE...
I'M ONLY SAYING THIS TO YOU...
KEEP THIS UNDER WRAPS, BUT...
...

THE CHURCH HALL CARETAKER

WILL WELCOME YOU WHEN YOU ARRIVE

DEACONS

FOR SOME, BEING A DEACON IS A STEPPING STONE TO BEING A PRIEST

TRAINING — DEACON — PRIESTHOOD

OTHER DEACONS ARE PERMANENT OR 'DISTINCTIVE' DEACONS

THEY DON'T PRESIDE AT COMMUNION OR GIVE THE BLESSING

THEY DON'T HAVE TO BE RESPONSIBLE FOR ALL OF THE BUILDINGS OR COMMITTEES

THIS MEANS THEY CAN SPEND MORE TIME WITH ACTUAL PEOPLE

AND GET INVOLVED IN THE LOCAL COMMUNITY AND ALL SORTS OF THINGS LIKE THAT

ADDITIONAL DRAWINGS, FOR WHICH YOU WILL NOT BE CHARGED EXTRA
↓

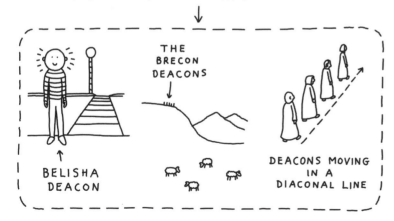

BELISHA DEACON

THE BRECON DEACONS

DEACONS MOVING IN A DIACONAL LINE

THEIR JOB IS TO BE A LINK BETWEEN THE CHURCH AND THE OUTSIDE WORLD

SO WHAT WAS THE VICAR'S SERMON ALL ABOUT THIS MORNING?

I HAVE ABSOLUTELY NO IDEA

ORDINATION PHOTOS

APPROVED POSES

ON A STAIRCASE

PUNCHING THE AIR

LEAPING

THROWING HATS
(MISTAKENLY
INCLUDED FROM
'GRADUATION' LIST)

PIGGYBACK/
MISCELLANEOUS
TOMFOOLERY

FORMAL, WITH THE BISHOP

THE NEW CURATE

A BINGO CARD - TICK OFF WHEN COMPLETED

QUOTES A CHURCH
FATHER IN A SERMON

GETS THE ARCHDEACON'S
NAME WRONG

SUCCESSFULLY ROBES
WITHOUT ASSISTANCE

"LET US JUST GO
BACK TO THE GREEK"

LOCKS THEMSELVES
OUT OF THE CHURCH

LOCKS THEMSELVES
IN THE CHURCH

GETS THEIR BOOKSHELVES
UP AND ORGANISED

MANAGES TO FIND
THE CREM

FILES THEIR FIRST
TAX RETURN

FORGETS INTERCESSIONS,
SO LEADS THEM SILENTLY

GETS LOST IN THE
LOCAL HOSPITAL

VISITS THE
WRONG PERSON

CURATES

THE MESS THEY LEAVE BEHIND WHEN THEY MOVE ON

SURPLUS CRAFT ITEMS,
COLLECTED BY THE
CONGREGATION FOR SIX MONTHS

A BIG PROJECT,
STARTED JUST
BEFORE THEY LEFT

THE AFTERMATH OF A
SERMON ILLUSTRATION THAT
WENT SLIGHTLY AWRY

NEW-FANGLED IDEAS
LEARNED AT
THEOLOGICAL COLLEGE

A LARGE INK STAIN
ON THE PRECIOUS
SERVICE REGISTER

A CONGREGATION
WHO WILL RATHER
MISS THEM

THE VICAR'S DAY OFF

WHAT PEOPLE THINK HAPPENS

LIE IN

BREAKFAST IN BED

LEISURELY INTERNET BROWSING

TAXI TO TOWN

LUNCH WITH FRIENDS

SHOPPING

MANICURE

POSH DINNER

THEATRE

TAXI HOME

WHAT ACTUALLY HAPPENS

PARISHIONER CALLS AT 7 AM

MAKING PACKED LUNCHES

ADMIN

FERRYING FAMILY MEMBERS

PHOTOCOPYING

COPIER BROKEN

WAIT IN FOR COPIER ENGINEER

COVER SERVICE FOR COLLEAGUE

COOK DINNER

COLLAPSE, EXHAUSTED

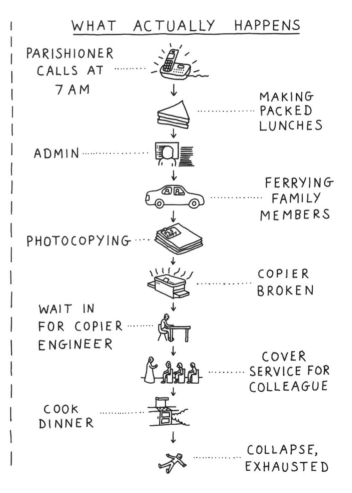

69

CLERGY DAYS OFF

WAYS PARISHIONERS ATTEMPT COMMUNICATION

E MAIL

GRAFFITI ON
NEIGHBOURING BUILDINGS

SKY WRITING

CARRIER PIGEON

FOLLOWING ON A
SOCIAL NETWORK

FOLLOWING IN
THE SUPERMARKET

DOOR-TO-DOOR
EVANGELISM

RURAL CLERGY

CHALLENGES FACED ON A SUNDAY MORNING

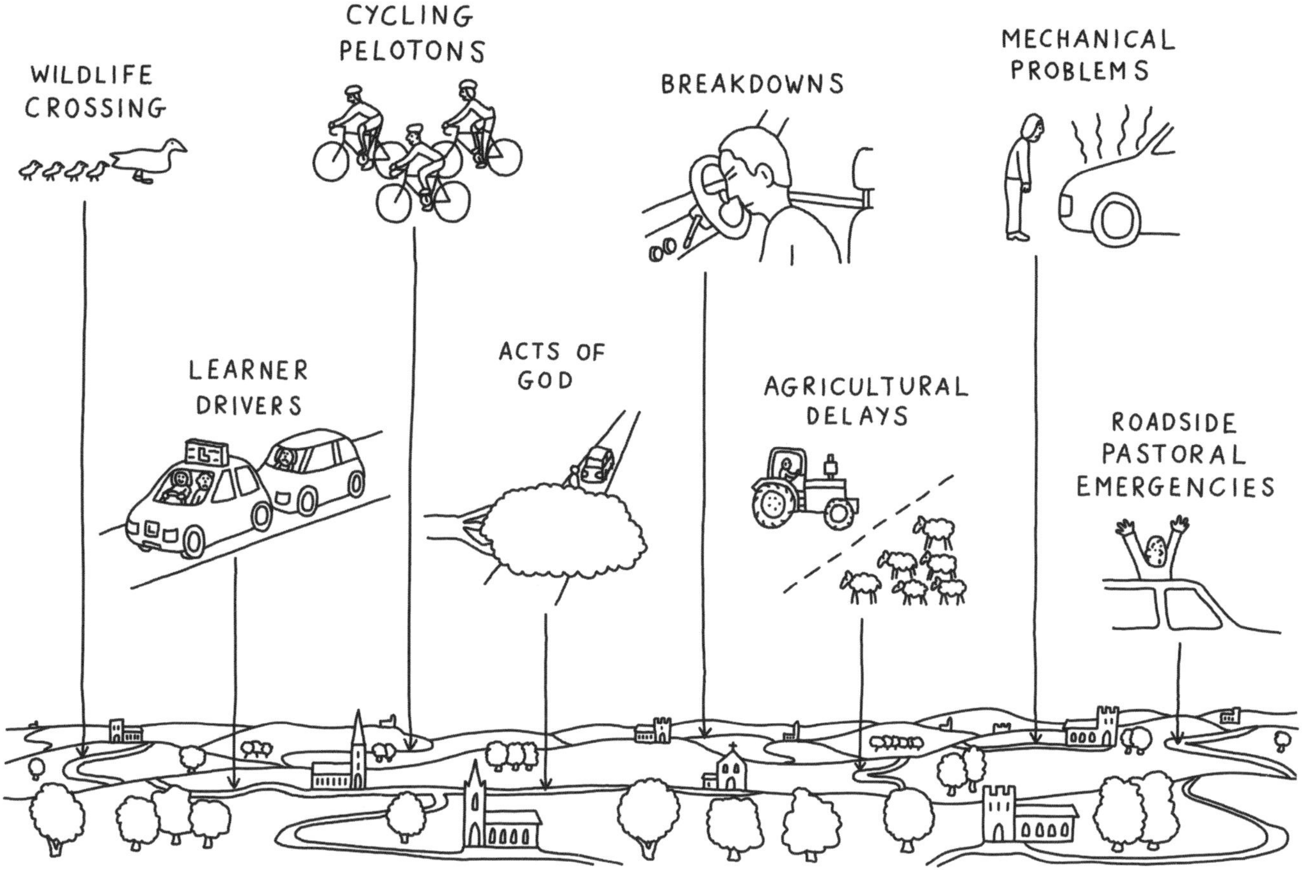
WILDLIFE CROSSING
CYCLING PELOTONS
BREAKDOWNS
MECHANICAL PROBLEMS
LEARNER DRIVERS
ACTS OF GOD
AGRICULTURAL DELAYS
ROADSIDE PASTORAL EMERGENCIES

VARIOUS ADVERSARIES

FACED BY THE CLERGY

VS.

NON-WELCOMING
WELCOMERS

DEAR VICAR,
I WAS DISAPPOINTED
TO SEE THAT

DISGRUNTLED
NEIGHBOURS

OBSCURED
ALTAR

FRENZIED
FLOWER
ARRANGERS

NO.

OVER-CAUTIOUS
TREASURERS

UP
DAT
ING

THE CHURCH
OFFICE
COMPUTER

I WANT
YOU TO
LOOK FOR
THE GRAVE

UNGENIAL
GENEALOGISTS

DISORGANISED
ORGANISTS

LETTERS
URGING
MORE
ACTION

THE
AUTHORITIES

WHY?

THE
INNER
VOICE

DON'T FORGET...

YOUR HYMN BOOK

THAT YOU'RE PREACHING AT THE 10AM

TO PUT OUT THE
ORANGE SQUASH CUPS

THE PASTORAL VISIT YOU
ARRANGED FOR THURSDAY

THE TELEPHONE

HOW CLERGY DEALT WITH IT BEFORE THE INVENTION OF THE ANSWERPHONE

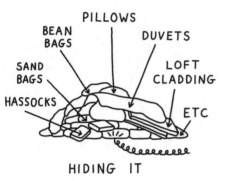

PILLOWS
BEAN BAGS
DUVETS
SAND BAGS
LOFT CLADDING
HASSOCKS
ETC

HIDING IT

I'VE NO IDEA WHERE HE IS I'M AFRAID

GETTING SOMEONE ELSE TO ANSWER

DISCONNECTION DEPT.

VICARAGE

STOPPING PAYMENT OF THE BILLS

¿DÍGAME?

PRETENDING TO BE OF A DIFFERENT NATIONALITY

EATING MEALS IN THE GARDEN

CUSHION

ELASTIC BAND

DULLING THE SOUND

EXASPERATED FAMILY

TAKING EVERY CALL

ACHES AND PAINS

COMMON DISEASES OF THE CLERGY

EAR ACHE

BAD BACK

HYPOCHONDRIA

AND LET ME TELL YOU ABOUT MY OTHER PROBLEM, VICAR

TENNIS ELBOW

LITURGICAL GESTURES

KNEE PAIN

KNEE-PROTECTORS (POSSIBLY AVAILABLE ONLINE)

HIGH TEMPERATURE

CONFESSING TO THE BISHOP

PETS
FOR CLERGY

DOGS

ALLOWING PASTORAL
ENCOUNTERS

CATS

AS PAPERWEIGHTS

PARROTS

HELPING REMEMBER
PEOPLE'S NAMES

GOLDFISH

FORGETTING DETAILS
OF THINGS HEARD
UNDER CONFESSION

TORTOISES

TO ASSIST WITH
TAKING A LONG
VIEW OF THINGS

ELEPHANTS

TALKING ABOUT THINGS
THAT NO ONE ELSE
IS MENTIONING

PASTORAL VISITING

WAYS THE CLERGY COPE WHEN THE TV IS LEFT ON

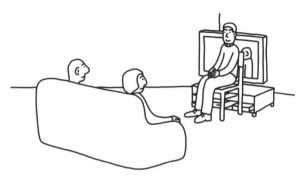

THE BLOCKER

THE JOINER

THE SPOILER

THE CELEBRANT

THE VICAR'S SPOUSE

THEIR RESPONSIBILITIES

KNOW THE VICAR'S SCHEDULE
FOR THE NEXT TWELVE MONTHS

ARRANGE FLOWERS AND/OR
PUT UP SHELVES

MAKE THE VICARAGE AVAILABLE
TO ALL CHURCH MEMBERS

TAKE DETAILED MESSAGES
ABOUT WEDDINGS AND FUNERALS

NOT BE SEEN TO BE
HAVING TOO MUCH FUN

BE ABLE TO LOCATE THE
VICAR AT ANY MOMENT

[ALSO: KNOW WHO EVERYONE IS; BE ABLE TO EXPLAIN THE VICAR'S SERMON; DO EVERYTHING
THE PREVIOUS VICAR'S SPOUSE DID; REFRAIN FROM EXPRESSING OPINIONS IN CHURCH GROUPS; TAKE
ROLES IN CHURCH GROUPS; UNDERSTAND HOW THE PHOTOCOPIER WORKS; MAKE THE TEA]

TO BE A BISHOP

THE QUALITIES REQUIRED

THE RIGHT EDUCATION

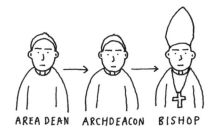

TO HAVE FOLLOWED THE
APPROPRIATE CAREER PATH

CHILDREN WITH
BIBLICAL NAMES

NOT SWEAR TOO MUCH, OR
SPEAK IN A REGIONAL ACCENT

A LOVE OF WALKING

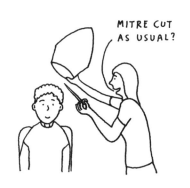

A SENSIBLE HAIRCUT

MITRES
ALTERNATIVE USES

 TEA COSY

 LAMPSHADE

 PUPPET

 HANGING BASKET

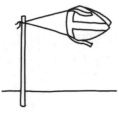 WINDSOCK

 PIPING BAG

 DIRECTION SIGN

 OVEN MITT

 COLLECTION BAG

 BUNTING

 WASTE PAPER BASKET

 KITE

 POPCORN HOLDER

 BASEBALL GLOVE

 BELLOWS

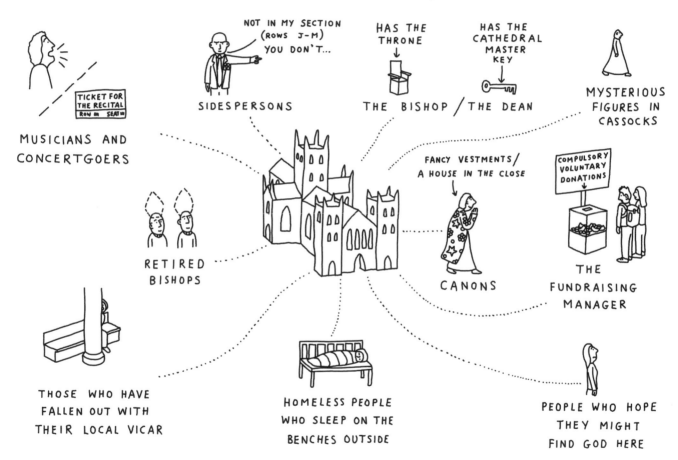

THE CATHEDRAL

THE PEOPLE YOU WILL FIND THERE

THOUGHT FOR THE DAY

THE VICAR IS ON
'THOUGHT FOR THE DAY'

PEOPLE SHE HOPES ARE LISTENING	PEOPLE WHO ARE ACTUALLY LISTENING

THE BISHOP

ALL HER SOCIAL MEDIA FOLLOWERS

SOMEONE DOING THE WASHING UP

A DELIVERY DRIVER

A TV TALENT SCOUT

HER MUM

A TENNIS FAN WITH TUNING DIFFICULTIES

AN INSOMNIAC USING THE RADIO TO GET TO SLEEP

THE REFORMATION

HOW WE ARE PLANNING TO CELEBRATE THE QUINCENTENARY

POSTING 95 NOTICES ON THE CHURCH DOOR

TEARING DOWN SUPERSTITIOUS IMAGERY

WHITEWASHING OVER THE YOUTH GROUP MURAL

CASTING OUT THE OHP

TAKING THE OPPORTUNITY TO QUIETLY DISPOSE OF THE STATUE OF THE PREVIOUS VICAR

A BRING-AND-SHARE LUNCH

REFORMED HAM

83

REMAIN OR LEAVE?

THE CHILDREN:

 OR

REMAIN IN THE SERVICE

LEAVE, AND GO TO THEIR
SUNDAY SCHOOL GROUPS

THE PREACHER:

 OR

REMAIN IN THE PULPIT

LEAVE THE PULPIT AND
WANDER AROUND WITH
THE MICROPHONE

SOME OF THE
CONGREGATION:

 OR

REMAIN AT THE PARISH CHURCH

NO VISITORS

PARISH SHARE

LEAVE AND FORM OUR OWN
CONGREGATION, DECIDE WHO CAN
JOIN, REJECT DIOCESAN BUREAUCRATS,
AND EASILY AFFORD A YOUTH
WORKER, FRESH COFFEE, ETC

THE BRING AND SHARE LUNCH

THE ELECTION

THE CHOSEN DATE IS NOT REALLY TERRIBLY CONVENIENT

WE HAVE THE
TODDLER GROUP
IN THE HALL ON
A THURSDAY

LIKELY SCENES:

BESIEGEMENT OF
THE POLLING CLERKS

REQUISITION OF THE
VOTING PENCILS

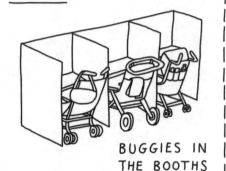

BUGGIES IN
THE BOOTHS

HARASSMENT OF
THE ELECTORATE

TRADITION

HOW IT DEVELOPS

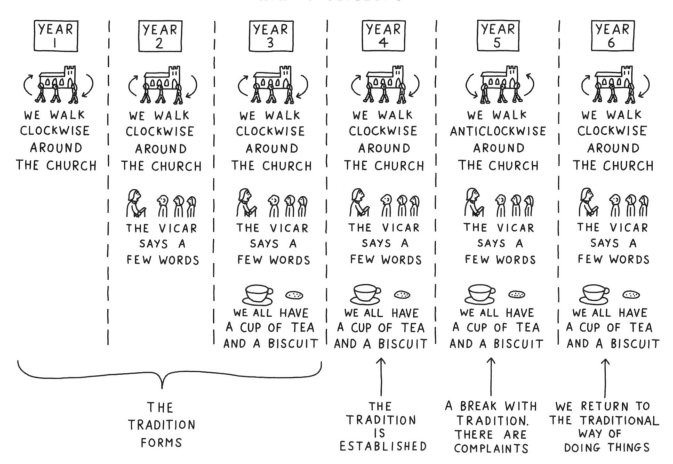

GEOLOGICAL PHENOMENA

OBSERVED IN CHURCH

EROSION

OF THE CONGREGATION OVER TIME

SEDIMENTARY FORMATION

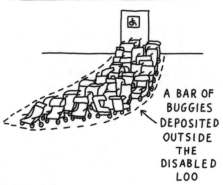

A BAR OF BUGGIES DEPOSITED OUTSIDE THE DISABLED LOO

GLACIATION

THINGS MOVING VERY SLOWLY (ESPECIALLY IN WINTER)

ERUPTION

PLATE TECTONICS

TRYING TO CARRY TOO MUCH FOR THE BRING-AND-SHARE LUNCH

SLUMP

TASKS

THAT WE COULD GET THE YOUTH TO DO

OPERATE THE
PROJECTOR

JOIN THE
COFFEE ROTA

MAINTAIN THE
CHURCH GARDEN

PLAN AND LEAD A
SPECIAL SERVICE

THIS IS
ALEX

SHE IS
THE
YOUTH

THE FLOWER ARRANGERS
EXACT THEIR REVENGE

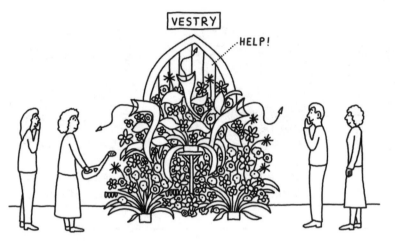

IMMOBILISATION OF THE CLERGY

REQUISITION OF
ECCLESIASTICAL
INSTRUMENTS

CAUSING A BIT OF A SCENE IN THE CAR PARK